Spiral Jibe's

GW00692239

PRIMAL
URGE

Spiral Jibe

Chris Clayton was educated at Shiplake College,
Henley-on-Thames and then spent three years at Havant
College in Hampshire.
His many influences and interests include: Blake, Byron,
Coleridge, Shelley, Aldous Huxley, Jim Morrison,
Shamanism, Philosophy, Psychology and most subjects
connected to developing the mind.
Whilst travelling in California he spent many months
high up in the Sierra Nevada Mountains. A chance
meeting with an Indian Shaman sparked a fascination
with the magic of lost tribal cultures and a yearning to
explore unknown regions of the mind. Many of his
poems in this book reflect leaps into those regions and
journeys beyond the realms of reality. He is currently
exploring the possibility of producing an album with the
other half of Spiral Jibe; Dylan Blight.

Dylan Blight was educated at the Portsmouth Grammar
School. He went on to Portsmouth Art College and
received a Diploma in Audio Visual Communications. He
currently runs a Holistic gift shop, Tattoo Studio and
Body Piercing Clinic.
He has lectured at colleges, made radio and television
appearances all in his quest to reveal the truth regarding
Britain's Ancient indigenous faith.
In 1993 he became the Arch Druid of the Insular Order of
Druids and he is also a member of the Council of British
Druid Orders.

For more information on Spiral Jibe write to:

Spiral Jibe
PO Box 20
Hayling Island
Hampshire
PO11 9TU

Please enclose a stamped addressed envelope.

Special thanks to:
John & Patricia Clayton, Granny Long, Marie Renée,
Angela Batchelor, Chris D'Costa, Deborah Clayton,
James Vanstone, Jane Adams, Alex Scott, Tim Loder,
Peter Clayton, Niki Henderson, Betty Osbourne,
Bishops, Labyrinth, China Sea Traders, all our friends
and everyone who gave us encouragement and support
during the production of this book.

Poems written by Chris Clayton (CC) and
Dylan Blight. (DB)

Cover Design from an original concept
by Chris Clayton and digitally illustrated by The Creator.

Posters by Chris Clayton.

Digital artwork, and typesetting by The Creator.

Hand drawn section illustrations by Jake Symmonds.

Promoters: The Arwen Brothers.

*"Revel in the power of the imagination
and free one's mind of all its restrictive conditioning"*
Spiral Jibe

Authors' Warning

Take full heed my reader dear
lest you become enchanted
the words within may seem quite queer
within your minds implanted

By power of word, and word alone
we set out to bewitch thee
within the safety of your home
we'll capture and enrich ye

So read our spells if you do dare
and enter now into our realm
And we will there your minds ensnare
with words of oak, ash, thorn and elm

We'll take you on the sweetest journey
for which you dream but have not taken
with us your minds will fly and tourney
and all your worries be forsaken

So read on, inspired, all of ye fain
into the lands where words are power
and never have their meanings plain
but glisten like a starlit shower

Your ears unto our tongues are tethered
by chains of finest satin gold
As shamans we your minds have feathered
as often did the bards of old.

love

The Wicked Lady

She slithers like a serpent,
She licks her rosey lips,
Her body slim and supple,
As she moves her curvey hips.

A wicked lady she may be,
I neither care nor think,
I raise my brimming glass,
And toast her with a drink.

My impure thoughts are her's,
I am her slave to be,
She is the wicked lady,
The seductress of me.

A servant true am I,
She's cast her wicked spell,
To be alone without her,
Is a sentence set in hell.

She feeds upon my innocence,
A pleasure I gladly give,
She is the wicked lady,
The one with whom I live.

Maiden so Fair

Maiden so fair I want you
I hope you are aware
for I cannot put into words
my hearts sweet love affair

For you, you know I'd gladly die
Of this you can be sure
The thoughts of love I have for you
taste sweet for they are pure

To be the one that cares for you
Someone who's always there
to serve my Goddess faithfully
Is my most heartfelt prayer

You stir my words to poems
and make me want to sing
So listen to these words of mine
and the lovesong that they bring

Your beauty it has weakened me
My thoughts are just of you
I really want you in my life
And hope you want me too.

Ode to Love

Love is found in a single flower,
In a drop of rain so clear,
Love is pure as the driven snow
In our hearts we hold so dear.

Love is all we seek to find,
In warm embrace we fear,
Love shall run away from us,
So soon will disappear.

Love is our sanctuary from the world,
We hide from all we see,
It teaches us we're human still
And all we long to be.

Love mingles, floats in such a way,
Love sings and thus it cries,
Love reigns above all else we feel
And beyond us when we die.

Catherines Eyes

A single look from Catherines Eyes
stirs around all my insides
It really is then no surprise
I wish I was between her thighs
Her legs slowly apart I'd prise
My mouth would then its tongue apply
and taste her place of Apple pies
and as she moans and sweetly sighs
that cosmic moment soon arrives
for giving thanks that we're alive
towards this end I'll always strive
for she's the queen of my bee hive
and without her I am deprived
and wonder if I will survive
my love for her will always thrive
for I have looked in Catherines Eyes.

She

She wandered in, she smiled so sweet
She always dressed so fine.
So pure both in her thought and dress
This flowering rose of time.

Her delicate moves, her perfect poise
I longed to see her too,
To hold her close against my chest
And share her love so true.

The fire that burns within my heart
She kindles with her breath,
I'll love her till the end of time
And beyond the realms of death.

"To Sarah and Lucy"

The pleasure that you give me
I cannot thank you more
For happiness seems easy
When your knocking at my door.

The smiles that you bring me
Seem so simple when their yours
What would I do without you
As my love for you just soars.

That special gift you gave me
I feed upon its core
For all the joy you gave me
I just love you more and more

The Life that lays before us
Has only just begun
Yet I know its one to savour
As we thrill in it as one.

A person's path is chosen
We choose it on our own
If we walk along the right one
A blissful life is grown

Surfice to say I thank you
You know I love you true
For all the special moments
I gladly spend with you.

Grey Eyes

She dances in a ring of fire,
Dampens the flames with her generosity of spirit
And raises the sun during the dark hours.
As the flowers in full bloom,
She excites the bee with her sweet scent.

Such joy, such abundence in warmth of character,
So much to release, so little to fear
Yet shaded by the shadow of youth.
An ember burning brighter than any star
And exuding the true nature of love itself.

Oh, such joy, such beauty, such love.

I am Thine

I am a man with my eye upon you
I am unstuck but you are my glue
I am a juggler with balls in the air
And this is a line of my magical prayer
I am a fortune a wealth to acrue
But I am a bowler whos struck out on you
I am an arrow aimed right at you
I am a problem but you are my clue
I am a wizard with words to a spell
But you're an enchanteress making me yell
I am a hero and you are my quest
I am a student but you are my test
I am a teacher and you are my class
But in this test it is me that must pass
I am a secret sworn not to tell
And I am a bard who is writing a spell
I am a hawk, but you are a dove
And I am a heart that is needing your love
I am a picture you've seen once before
My name is Justice but you are my law
I am a hunter and you are a fox
Your hair is golden sweet curly locks
I am a breeze and I'm wafting your hair
But you are a goddess making me stare
I am a Cauldron cooking up stews
I am a poet but you are my muse.
I am so close that I'm making you tremble
And I am a priest, but you are my temple
I am a tattoo, but you are my skin
I am a mouth, but you are my grin

I am a pool player, but you are my cue
And I am a song and I am sung just to woo
You are a sleep and I am your bed
And I am a thought and I'm inside your head
I am on "Waynes World" and you are my babe
And I am a sinner who never forgave
I am a treasure but you are my chest
Of all would be lovers I am the best
I am a dragon and you are my tail
I am a knight and you are my grail
I am a sword and I'll be your shield
I'll bend in the wind if only you'll yield
I'm on a journey and you are my path
I am a pilgrim and you are my staff
I am an alchemist, you are my stone
I am a King, but you are my throne
You are clay whilst I am just mud
But I am a vampire sucking your blood
I am flesh and you are my bones
I am a reader but you are my tomes
I am a street, but you are my town
I am undressed, but you are my gown
Who am I ? Why I am thine
The question is will you be mine ?

Alternative Ending

Who am I ? Your Valentine
The question is will you be mine ?

Love Conquers All

Unboundless love the catalyst
Anton soldier'd through thickening mist,
A scowl he wore upon his face
Marching on at warriors pace.
A cry for help! It pierced the dark,
Guiding the blind swiftly to his mark.
He dashed forth to the wretched victim,
Ye Gods! He stumbled upon a limb
Of some hapless maid who wandered by
Unmindful of the lawful cry,
To appraise all folk, 'Madman escaped!
Take heed all women, or you'll be raped!'
Alone, cold and dreadfully weary
Anton sighed, relieved, the face was not the one of Keeri.

The dark crept in, he searched and searched to no avail
Then from the darkness came the beast
Sweaty , foul stinking all stillness ceased;
Bloodshot eyes a piercing stare
The moon lit up the demons glare,
A sweeping cowl dripped in blood
The fearful beast was human cud.
He raised his sword, brought it down,
Slicing through the skin and gown.
A screech of pain, the beast slashed out,
Anton's choice was death or rout.
Once more he caught this vile devil
A deathly blow, one which to revel.
The beast lunged forward too slow to gain
The killing blow was sure to reign.
Victorious in favour of Anton's might,
The beast was dead, he'd won the fight.

As for Keeri, she was found
Alive and well, yet tightly bound.
Anton and Keeri later wed
Pledged of safety now the beast was dead.

Of their love, it conquered all
A life of bliss in heaven's hall.

the universal

Jim Morrison

Dedicated to Liz, one of the few true rebels.

The Slippery serpent
A ride to the end
A magical tour
The Guardian did send.

Awoken by simplicity,
Enlightened by life;
A literary expression,
Cut by a knife.

Unsure horizons
Tainted by pills
Drugs sex and drink,
A vacation of thrills.

The unknown soldier,
Shot into fame;
Words came easy,
Notoriety mamed.

An incitor of riots
Self destructive in art;
A tragedy of words,
The end was the start.

Early on a Sunday Morning

Early on a Sunday morning
late infact I should be yawning
so why is it that I here write
so strange a way to spend the night
Why is it that you talk through me
is it so others too may see
The glorious vision of thee beholden
in the glades of grasses golden
Of maidens rainbows end perceives
within the heart that does not grieve
Of mothers pining for their child
with gentle looks that seem so mild
Of ancient wisdom in the crones song
which carries all our hearts along
Back to the cradle of formation
thanks to you sweet Inspiration

An Image

Show me good times,
Show me bad;
Take my innocence,
Make me glad.

The awakening comes,
Time for a show;
The curtains are up,
The lights are aglow.

Twisting and turning
Pulsing with lust;
Gyrating young thighs,
No sign of a bust.

Dense curling smoke,
Lit by the lights;
Smiling young faces
Aware of their rights.

Freedom's a word
They all understand;
Living for life,
Electric young band.

The lizard king cometh,
Exuding much risk;
Descending to levels,
That never exist.

Freedom of mind,
Lead by excess;
The slippery serpent,
A business success.

Words of a Poet - Part One

The words of the poet are a double edged sword
poetic and lyric they'll strike every chord
They sever the veil of our minds understanding
and penetrate truths that are oh so demanding

They fly through the air like the arrows of sun
and bite on their target when travel is done
Invoking the forces of metre and rhyme
to convey to you thoughts that are really sublime

They flow from the grail of all inspiration
And tell us of tales from Gods glorious nation
Giving us succour with great imagery
the words of the poet like leaves of a tree

They shield and protect us from numbing of brains
enriching our senses with each new refrain
But always remember the words that they tell
are beyond simple rhymes, my friends they are spells.

Words of a Poet - Part Two

The sword that they are will cut through illusion
with edge razor sharpened by their allusions
but we should not think of this as intrusion
for it is an end to the heart of delusions

They're arrows of truth shedding light on their path
when held onto tightly these arrows are staffs
Wands with to conjure, tools of the craft
The muses sharp wit is befashioned a haft

They taste oh so sweet they are music to ear
and are like a rudder emotions to steer
On a boat of thought cast loose from the pier
and words to describe them are simply to mere

So listen intently to words of the poet
Words that are ancient and possibly stoic
They may be a spell but they hold no trick
Just words of a poet not the words of old nick

A Wounded Child

Her tiny face
Swollen and sore,
So sad a tale
Of teeth that tore.

A tale of time
Time to heal,
The mental scars
Of her ordeal

Screams of pain
and terror within,
The snarling dog
Was sure to win

Cut and bruised
A sorrowful sight,
A wounded child
It is not right

We never learn
We always wait,
A tragedy occurs
We act too late.

Warnings were given
Yet swept aside,
A child disfigured
Torn apart inside.

Season of the Rose

Friendship's gown is as the rose
In full bloom it radiates love,
A blanket of warmth
To cover all chills
And flutters in the air as the dove.

In Summer it grows
Like flowers and trees,
In Autumn it begins to withdraw,
But in Winter it shrivels
And in Spring it doth heal
Then in Summer it blooms once more.

Woe the Pain

Oh the pain of being alone
Woe - the pain that won't go away
The pain within the inner heart
that still beats in the land of Logres
A pain felt standing on the sand
A pain felt walking in the trees
The pain of the hills, the streams, the waters,
The pain that causes hearts to grieve
Woe- the pain that wont go away

Orgy

In dedication to (un)certain political figures

Stockings suspenders
Bondage and gear
Lesbians, prostitutes,
Black leather queer.

Chains and man'acles,
Whips on the floor;
Enormous beds,
'Do Not Disturb' on the door.

Squealing she rose,
A lash was enough;
The whip was fun,
The chains too rough.

The mistress cometh,
A wicked young thing;
I paid her money,
Took off my ring.

Plucky young lads,
Prancing around;
Vile old sluts,
A hideous sound.

Sweat and saliva,
Panting and pain;
An orgy of lust,
Utterly insane.

Waking Moments
Nightmares

I wish only to dream of you
my waking moments nightmares
Sleep eludes me, slips away
I pursue it eagerly
like a hunter chasing a white deer
through ancient forests oh so dark

I want it so much
and yet the strength of my wish
creates barriers for my mind
obstacles, great hurdles
preventing me, torturing my soul.

Sleep, rest, tranquillity
will they ever be mine.
My mind swims like
the salmon of wisdom
a taste of which
brings forbidden knowledge
to one who knows all things

Like a serpent
sleep moves away
the more I try
the more awake I feel

My mind is hazy now
my pillow takes on new form
It feels like hair and velvet clothes
with you inside
I clutch tightly, holding on
I wish only to dream of you
my waking moments nightmares.

Time To Grow Up

The time for growing up is here
At any time we wish a beer,
We are not children plain to see
Mature enough to vote for thee,
So lets all think a little more
In changing laws we all deplore.

Wisdom

We see what the blind man cannot see.
The blind man hears what we cannot hear.

Death and Destruction

Death and destruction
So quick a pace,
All thank you to
The human race.

The Key To All

Words are the wisdom
Words are the pain
Words are the trigger
That drives you insane.
Words are the key
Words are the lock
Words are the door
Be sure you knock!

Stable Elections

"Manners maketh Man"
Was not it said
Politicians seem succumbed
To sheer rudeness instead.

A country lead by thugs
A sad old tale
Of arrogance, self-indulgence,
A vile concoction in the pale.

Naivety beds ingnorance
A mind seduced by conceit,
The dinner party of the fools
The stables should they meet.

Fingers in the pot of gold
All too greedy it is true,
A shameless pack of imbeciles
Not an uttered word is new!

We beg for new horizons
Yet I fear it not to be,
In the world of politicians
The ones who cannot see.

The Sharp Blade of Desire

Inspired by the death of Freddy Mercury

The end be sure
To whom the deathly fingers touch,
But in a state of mere lust
The Chancer dances on the sharp edge
Of a fine knife.

Balancing on the tightrope of tears,
Fallen heroes, idols of spurious meaning.
All seems possible!
All seems innocent!

One slip, one careless twinkling,
The Chancer like the warrior
Risks all, for what?

The sense of joy, of pleasure to be sure,
Yet controlled, with disquiet,
One's solace would be more and more.
Knowledge of the blade,
The acuteness of its perilous edge,
As one frolics with desire.

The Chancer may care to dance with desire,
Yet will he waltz with death?

Transvestite

Dear old fellow,
How do you do?
Long time since,
I last saw you.

You've changed somewhat,
I'm sure that's true.
A lady's figure,
How very nice too.

Dinner at eight,
You care to come?
Myself, a couple,
It should be fun.

A gay old evening,
That will be.
You'll gladly come,
I hope to see.

As for dress,
Of course you may;
No one will notice,
I dare say.

1990's,
Times have changed;
Faces, figures,
All re-arranged.

So please feel free,
To flaunt your wear;
As man or lady,
I neither care.

Morrisons Quest

Four letter words,
A dream like state;
Tainted inner vision,
A glimpse of his fate.

Searching for meaning,
Dabbling with life,
Bored of the pleasures,
On the edge of a knife.

Middle class grooming,
A rebel with cause;
Lost in the maze
And beaten by laws.

A guru of rock
Shrouded in mystery;
A young guy on drugs
Whose gone down in history.

Command of the language,
A knowledge of books;
Too bright for the rock world,
A rabble of crooks.

No to commercialism,
An artist too true;
Forced in the limelight,
Disappearing from view,

Eager for enlightment,
A hunger to learn;
The meaning of life,
An answer we yearn

The end came soon,
He died early on;
His question was answered,
Society was wrong.

Black Kittens Candle Light

Black kitten by the candles light
with fur so dark and eyes so bright
You sit and watch the shadows dance
as if you were in some deep trance
A silhouhette of darkness you
experiencing this strange happening new
You flit and skip across the floor
chasing nothings out the door
Your ears they twitch at every sound
the darkness gathers all around
around you on this darkest night
your fur so dark your eyes so bright
You seem to blend well in the dark
our only light a tiny spark
A candles flame within this room
is all that holds back utter gloom
A candles flame and you yourself
purring noises from your mouth
At having found new games to play
within this candle light so grey
You come and sit upon my book
I write this poem and you just look
Amazed at what I seem to do
and I'm it seems amazed by you
My kitten by the candles light
with fur so dark and eyes so bright.

And then you fall within your water
as your young legs do seem to falter
and backwards walking shake your legs
to cast off those unwanted dregs
Now climbing through the videos
with claws outstretched from nimble toes
Great darkness in a lesser dark
you sit and watch that single spark
that flickers light all round this room
and beats back all the close set gloom
My kitten by the candle light
with fur so dark and eyes so bright.

Bollocks

"Feels good if you read it out loud"

Bollocks to the selfish ones!
Bollocks to them all!
Bollocks to the politicians
Whose brains are rather small.

Bollocks to our Prime Minister!
Bollocks to his men!
Bollocks to the petty laws!
That apply to us not them.

Bollocks to the establishment!
Bollocks to them all!
Bollocks to the way they work!
Just wait and see them fall.

Bollocks is a lovely word!
Bollocks is how we feel!
Towards those ignorant fascists
Who rob and cheat and steal.

Bollocks is what we say to them!
Bollocks is our tool!
By reading this out loud
You'll feel better after all.

So shout it when you're feeling down
Shout **bollocks** to them all!
Bollocks to the government!
Then smile and watch them fall.

The Labourer's Lesson

Oh, bugger me!
Look at that girl!
Long and slender,
Lips that curl.

She saunters past,
A skirt so short;
"Lovely legs"
I do retort

She turns her head,
In disgust;
"Piss off bitch"
T'was only lust.

She turns again,
Strolls up to me;
Knees me hard;
"What a lovely knee".

I doubled up,
"That was nice";
But next time,
I'll think twice.

the mystical

Sacred Secret Fires Light

Sacred secrets sworn at night
by thy sacred fires light
Bring us closer to our source
the sacred serpents rivers course
From Goddess to the soul within
that tiny spark that shines so dim
Within the blackness of mans heart
can still be found that tiny part
that ever is and was of thee
Open our eyes that we might see
Don't let us in the darkness walk
Inspire our lips that we might talk
Of sacred secrets sworn at night
by thy sacred fires light.

Dance of the Shaman

A fiery spirit rises
From the ashes, cloaked
In words and seduced
By the rich tapestry
Of sound and rhythm

They seek him here
They seek him there
They will not find
The Shaman's lair

It's deep within
It's deep without
The Shaman's lair
Is all about

High up in hills
Deep in wood
The Shaman dances
In cape and hood

You hear him chant
You hear him sing
The Shaman knows
Your fears within

He sees within
With eyes without
So heed his words
They are devout

A ring of fire
A mound of earth
The Shaman soars
From death to birth

He knows who's in
He knows who's out
The Shaman's knowledge
Has power and clout

The trees his friends
The river blood
The night his home
The day his Love

You seek him here
You seek him there
You will not find
The Shaman's lair

He rises high
Above the rest
To show the way
Till all are blest

He's pure and clear
So dear and true
The Shaman guides
The way for you

You see without
He sees within
With eyes without
He lets you in

The Words do fly
The Words he sings
The Words of the Shaman
Fly With Wings

As quick as light
As soft as snow
He nurtures all
Those seeds you sow

The guise he wears
He knows of too
Unlike the rest
Has purpose through

In which to mould
And sculpt beyond
The slight of hand
A Shaman's wand

So seek him not
He'll come to you
In brightest colours
And fiery hue

He'll dance and sing
He'll twist and turn
With a wild shrug
To those who spurn

He's coming soon
I hear him now
Behold! He's here
No need to bow

No need to seek
No need to look
He is the Shaman
You'll know his look

With words of wisdom
And power within
He'll change your life
Without, Within

So dance and dance
The Shaman's song
It flows to you.
From ages long

He sings the song
He writes the words
The Shaman's sound
So like the birds

Is sung with rhythm
Is sung with care
The Shaman's smile
The Shaman's glare

He's coming here
He's coming there
The Shaman's voice
Is everywhere

So clear your mind
And wake up too
The dance of the Shaman
Is coming for you !

Mystic Quest

For Mystic union of man and God
there is a path the ancients trod
It went via moon and then by sun
their cosmic questing was begun
The seekers quest was high and lonely
The shamans drum became his pony
To reach the stars and be as one
with all creation under sun
And now you are a seeker too
and to that path you must be true
Enlightenment will come to thee
and shine from you for all to see
But first you must know of the path
and walk that road with hermits staff
The journey is of course within
along a path that seems too thin
Then having fed on cosmic food
that heroes and the gods have chewed
A holy communion with the self
to heal the ails of psychic health
Then further on this path to tread
from man to god on silver threads
The river of our inspiration
flowing from Gods most gratious nation

Into the world where we do dwell
the place known by some as hell
And they you'll find a great Abyss
the point of which you must not miss
Only the one who knows his worth
can cross this gap with gleeful mirth
For then your mind will be expanded
no further sacrifice demanded
Just union with the force supreme
and all the levels in between
To reach and wear the crown of Kether
and realise your life is better
And then return to mortal realm
to wear this knowledge like a helm
This is the way to consciousness
and always was the mystics quest
You're not alone for it is true
that other seekers reach there too
They are the ones of inner light
the ones of mercy and of might
They have been the great magicians
who've taught this quest in their traditions
And now the journeys up to you
so please don't of this path eschew
Become as one with them of old
and never say you were not told !

Mirror Image

A demon sang a song of pity,
Tormented souls within the city.

Distant, floating, he wept with joy,
A lamentable life, a mere boy.

Angular fiend who feeds on love
Bedevilled by good, a snow white dove.

All good seen is one man's evil,
Adrift in time, God's holy easel.

Dreams

During my sleep one night,
I drifted to a far off land,
Dakariah and Fucalon,
Manors of a golden sand.

I glided high up in the sky,
I drifted through puffy white cloud ,
Dakariah and Fucalon,
Gleaming cities of ice blue cold.

I gazed at the soaring buildings,
Reaching high up in the sky,
Dakariah and Fucalon,
Realms where I wish to die.

I followed the rivers of silver,
From their end to the Oceans of lead,
Dakariah and Fucalon,
Dominions where money is red.

I passed a religious ceremony,
Not a church but a huge arena,
Dakariah and Fucalon,
A place where times are meaner.

I saw God on many occasions,
Worshipped by most as a lover,
Dakariah and Fucalon,
Where money is the God and the Lover.

I awoke that very same night,
Back home from my journey so long,
Dakariah and Fucalon,
A journey I feel is wrong.

The Subconscious Mind

As black as night
As black as blind,
The darkness of
Subconscious mind.

A journey through
An endless ride,
Obey strict rules
You must inside.

The abyss consumes
All that waver,
Be sure of why,
Or meet your saviour.

Many hidden secrets
Long since lost,
Missing in action,
Our society's cost.

Pilgramage, Odyssey,
Travel or trek,
"Tread carefully, dear brother',
One's mind you could wreck.

Run away memories
Assassins of thought,
Negative thinking,
Kill before caught.

Whizzing at speed
Tearing down space,
An infinite number,
Time and musing in race.

A cosmos contained
A universe of will,
The powers of life,
The powers to kill.

Nourshed on trivia
Fed by the spoon,
Tides of negativity,
Short tales of gloom.

Abscond from the wastelands
A graveyard of dross,
Lay mind to a leader
Who died on the cross.

History and Time
Veiled in hell,
A destiny for those
Who think from a shell.

Mysteries unveiled,
Voyages nocturnal,
Our subconscious mind,
A voyage eternal.

In Raven Darkness

In Raven darkness, sweet embrace
clings softly as a velvet claw
scratching at your flesh
sends shivers down your spine
cascading through your body
making you mine

Your eyelids feeling heavy
bombarded by the light
too hectic for the night
You close them gently
wishing yourself asleep
but holding on to wakefullness
afraid to go too deep

My fingers sending tendrils
of ecstacy and fear
trembling echoes of a dream
almost remembered
And yet slipping in
and out of consciousness
out of sight and out of mind

Waves of desire
held back with care
and watching so intently
with eyes all aglair
Piercing your sinews
reaching deep inside
your mind is open now
filled with my presence
waiting for tommorrow,
and what might be

Stillness, fading ripples
on the surface of a lake
Blood dripping hotly
into a pool of swirling dreams
Thoughts reaching out,
wrapping you in a cloak
In Raven darkness - sweet embrace
clings softly as a velvet claw.

Stones Fear

Great lake of Poets words is still
Is still amongst us beyond the hill
The hill of all our mental blocks
That blocks the flow with stubborn locks
That locks away from us the keys
The keys for writing Poetries
Poetries that we all wish to write
To write and share within this night
This night we all will be inspired
Inspired, uplifted and required
Required to sing to thee our Praises
Praises that our stones fear raises.

Druid Mystics

Druid Mystics then abounded
In you alone their faith was founded
Then as now so few perceived
thy light wihtin the darkness grieved
Your passion was the ecstacy
Of Oak and Ash and Thorn and tree
creatures all around were tethered
be they smooth or furred, or feathered
To your worship they all advanced
dancing then thy sacred dance
Singing then your worthy praises
that serpent consciousness a'raises
To once again return to grace
and worthy be before thy face
And poets voice you then commanded
Within our hearts your seed was planted
Let it grow within again
that we may be as we were then
Seasons, time and minutes passed
surely we are not the last
Nor the first to think this way
And as thy children out to play
Within our modern world so vast
so much hatred has been cast
That you're afraid we will not listen
to the words of your tradition
But Gia we are now aware
And know and will keep silent dare
To live the way you would desire
and take our consiousnesses higher

That we may live within thy light
and dance around thy fires bright
And sing again your age old praises
within this world so full of crazys
May Druid Mystics still be found
when your voice has lost its sound ?
Its sound that brings us closer to thee
When we sing our poet - ery
Do you listen to our voices
as we run out of our choices
Help us find our true vocation
bardic priests within thy nation
A breed of warriors we will be
and always we will fight for thee
for truth and justice and worthy cause
we'll fight with tooth and nail and claws
to be the guardians of your faith
and in your guiding light so stayeth
As Druid Mystics we will abound
until thy holy grail be found.

Heaven or Hell

The sword of God slashed in the sky,
He spat his wrath, proceeded by the cry
Of doom that spread such terror,
A foreboding of mere mortal error.
To all who heeded this heavenly warning
Woke contented in the morning.
Those foolish one's of narrow vision
Gaping mouths who would not listen,
Fouled God's garden once too often,
Joined the ranks of all that's rotten.

Water danced in tune with lead,
Pastures green were concrete fed,
Rain that turned the green to brown,
Man's self-indulgence, yet natures gown.
A robe of sin for man to wear,
For all the times he did not care
To stop and muse upon his way,
Of blackening even the brightest day.
A trait of man he cannot quell,
As heaven dies creating hell.

Yet if direction changes soon,
Songs in heaven could be his tune.
Fields of lush, deep green grass,
Seas of life in time would pass.
Creation slowly seen advancing;
Destruction ceased, all life enhancing.

Tir-Na-Nog

Land of youth, tir-na-nog
fabled island in the west
Since I first heard your name
desire I've held to be your guest
And search all through your ancient forests
where time stands still and suns don't set
And drink your hazel clear springwater
and thereof inspiration get
I'd like to ride on your wild horses
which fly at will cross earth and sky
Hear my hearts plee now oh Goddess
draw me in before I die.

Good and Evil

The warrior marched forward with steel at his side
Driven by the force from the love of his bride.
Intent on destroying the beast whom he knew
Had stolen his love like the sun takes the dew.

This creature of darkness spread terror in its wake
As the ripples of evil on the banks of the lake;
Devoid of all goodness this fiend who he saw
Came slashing and spitting like Beelzebub's whore.

Thunder, his brother, the earth did he shake
With vast fingers of fire he slashed in his wake.
Dear Heaven awoke from a slumber so long
Unable to banish this colossus of wrong.

Wild demons of vengeance hellbent on a kill
Spewed out from the earth and charged down the hill.
Fire, water, brimstone and blood
The daughters of Satan rose up from the mud.

The water turned crimson, the sky jet black
As darkness swept in, on the wings of a bat.
The ground was shaking, a gale did blow
And the spawn of the Devil continued to grow.

Our Defender of Life fought back with his soul
Believing in life, love and his role,
As Guardian of Earth his quest incomplete
Till the Devil bows down before Life's rightful seat !

Shamans Odes

Oh to fly on eagles wings
to the land of Tir-nan-Og
To where Rhiannons birds do sing
within the minds vast crannog

Oh to swim that dark abyss
enshrouded in our otters furs
and somehow there discover bliss
within the cauldron, Cerridwen stirs.

Oh to reach the sacred mountain
the pinnacle of our desires
built around our fire gods fountain
so hidden by the quoggy mires

Oh to find Old Wayland Smith
our souls reforged by dwarven hammer
thus changing our essential - pith
yet deafened not by all their clamour

Oh to ride on Shamans drum
to dance quite naked round the fires
serpents rising from basal skum
living out our hearts desires.

Oh to climb the shamans ladder
rising though our consciousness
spiral dances make us madder
giving us the power to bless

Oh to find our spirit guidance
from animal forms veneered within
to journey will-bourne in trance
to that land devioid of sin.

Rhyme of the Ancient Mystic Maid

There was an Ancient mystic maid
who danced among the stones upraised
by ancient giants and called the dance
who seemed to move as if entranced

She seemed to hear the unheard voices
presenting me with many choices
Whispers softly through her brain
and faeries shouting out her name

She ran around the stones great circle
in her gown of green and purple
flecked about with amber drops
the citrine of her curly locks

It seemed that many silver bands
adorned the fingers of her hands
It seemed that many blue bells rang
And in my head it seemed she sang

She sang a song of ancient altars
that caused my hearts strong beat to falter
A song that seemed to wail right through me
A song of love about or to me.

This truly ancient mystic maid
with whom when young I think I played
whilst picknicking on Salisbury plain
I'm sure I heard her call my name.

The goddess of the stones is she
that seems so young and truly free
that hates the fences and the wires
surrounding all her free desires

She wanders there four times a year
and thinks the guards in black so queer
She's never seen so strange a sight
as those who guard her through the night

And keep out all the travelling hippies
the stoned, the drunk, or truly trippies
Who else with her would dance and sing
and all their heavy clothes off sling
Could she be that famed "belle dame"
that lures men out of hearth and home
And makes them dance all through the night
around her sacred stones so bright.

This truly ancient mystic maid
with whom when young I think I played
And cast with her so many spells
for love and truth - I know she yells,

I know she'd rather have no chains
locking up our foddered brains
But torcs of gold round all our necks
that glisten like the starlit flecks

Of amber in her citrine locks
as she dances around the blocks
Of sacred blue stones in the night
and parties on as is her rite

A rite that we're denied this day
as with our friend we want to play
but she's shut in and we're shut out
even though we are devout

Devout, devoid now of our maid
who dances still where once I played
whilst picknicking on Salisbury plain
I'm sure she calls to me by name.

Song of the Stones

Power
Power of the Stones
Rising from the Earth
Cascading down as light
from the myriad stars
that speckle nights cloak

Great Sol rises sedately
casting her eye on the revelers within
Drumbeats pulse and fill the air
and strange music lingers there
Voices chanting, drummers drumming
Druids dancing, singing wisdom
in the lyrics of their song
Women weaping - tears of pleasure
all - in the glory of the sun

Satyrs piping and a leaping
over virgins on the ground
mother goddess all around us
in the presence of this sound

Summer Solstice day of pleasure
joy to be there Singing praises
as the year begins to wane

Big wheel turning tears to laughter
in the circle of the mother
impregnated by the light
Seeds to carry ever onwards
planting oak trees of delight.

The Dark One

As darkness descends
A flicker of light,
Some distance away
An awesome sight.

The demon devours
All in its path,
Stripped of their flesh,
Ripped in half.

The gnashing of teeth
The slashing of claws,
The hideous beast
As death toll soars.

Born on the Sabbath
Repulsed by all good,
Shrouded by darkness,
A cape and a hood.

Lock up your children
Take to the hills,
The wicked one cometh,
Terror instills.

Wise and wicked
Wanton and weird,
Conjured by Goblins,
The dark one they feared.

As daylight approached
Darkness took flight,
The peasants returned,
With evil in sight.

He vomited forth
Gestated in hell,
The dark one forsakes,
Life for his shell.

The Pain of Pleasures Sadness

A goddess dances in a ring of fire
the rhythm of her feet sends shockwaves
cascading wildly through my soul.
The flames of desire are kindled
setting my head afire with smoke
Her movement suck me closer
I'm powerless to resist
onward ever onwards
she beckons with a kiss
Her softly yeilding lips
transport me to another world
which opens into starlight
upon a garden path
through many shades and colours
vague thought forms of futures that may never be
until I see her temple - standing alone and free

But the Goddess is a spider
a weaver of deceit
drawing in poor flies like me
with the pounding of her feet
The strands of her web are tangled
confused and out of place
theres pain within her heart
and there's sadness on her face.
Her temple has a guardian
a maiden - oh so fair
with spiders always weaving
tangled cobwebs in her hair

"I'm sorry faithfull follower - you'll have to go away
The Goddess isn't in her place
Theres no worshipping today."

"Oh, but can't I enter in - I come with noble cause
to offer living sacrifice beyond your temple doors."

Within the temple there is chaos
the insides messed around
Theres a screaming, theres a crying
theres a most unholy sound

"Oh, sweet and bitter Goddess
Why must you struggle so ?
Go fishing with your web of dreams
a surely you must know
Spiders as well as flies must drown
in the deep waters of emotion."

The acolite turns away to go - not understanding why
Without the sacred in his life
he knows that he must die
In pleasure she finds sadness
in her body only shame
she plays a wicked game alone
a fatal solitaire of pain
the pain of pleasures sadness
she's known in times before
And she can only turn and flee
when lust comes to her door.

Shape Shifters

They shift their shape
They shed their skin
The Shape Shifters cometh
They come from within

They come from within
They come from without
Wrap on new skin
Let the old shrivel out

Fly like the wind
Soar like the hawk
Run like a leopard
Shift as you talk

Silent and Quick
As fast as the light
The Shape Shifters cometh
With fire and might

You know not their names
You know not their look
As quick as you know
Your skin they have took.

So be on your guard
And hope for a sign
The Shape Shifters miss you
And vanish in time.

Prayer to the Goddess of Inspiration

Inspirer of an older time
I invoke thee to be mine
Bring to me thy dreams of truth
Open up the land of youth
Let me in to be thy friend
and start a new unbitter trend
Let thy people free once more
to walk with you beyond the door
of our perception let us be
united in thy unity
To be as one with tree and stone
and know that we have found our home

Age Old Inspirer
hearken now to our desire
to be again as one with thee
and ever then a blessed be
Our wish is pure as it is true
so send to us thy ancient clues
So we may walk again with thee
and know once more that we are free
We lost the way it must be told
a lack of interest in the old
ways that were once the norm
ways fresh out of pleasure born
Bring back to us thy ways eternal
encapsulate within a kernel
A sacred nut of wisdom make
that we again may pleasure take
Forever in thy Peace to dwell
beyond the realms of Christian Hell
Bring back to us thy pagan times
for in this wish there are no crimes
Our heart and soul cry out the thee
so please don't ever hide from we
Your people on this planet now
who've raped your earth with mutinous plough
and dug up all your sacred spaces
leaving few and far the traces
of that wisdom so desired
forgetting that we were inspired
of old as we are now by thee
return again that is our plea.

– DB –

A Damsel Dipped In Potion

In fairy land,
A man did stand
Upon a sacred place
Where Kara, Queen of all this land
Brought smiles to his face.

She danced the tune of all his love
She danced to his appeal
She sang the song of innocence
So finely clothed in zeal.

Beyond the mound
from where he stood
An ancient voice he heard,
Enchanted so it seemed to be
T'was nature Kara stirred.

Her flowing hair ! Those flasing eyes !
And all of nature stood to stare
Behold ! Behold !
You see her there
You see her fertile motion
She is the Queen of all this land
A damsel dipped in potion.

A distant realm
The land he trod
He loved her more and more,
Yet bound by chains of unseen force
He stumbled down in awe.

In stymie state
He sang to her
He sang with all his might,
He sang of all his love for her
as light devoured night.

Kara, Kara, oh so bright
Lead me out into the light,
Seek me out
Let me in
Leave me not alone to sin

She smiled sweet
Upon these sounds
She smiled with occaision
Alas t'was only merriment
Spurred on by dulcet motion.

Jaded by this slight dismissal
Hungry for her time
He sang again a tune for her
To try and change her mind

Kara, Kara, Queen of time
Please listen to my heartfelt rhyme
I sing for you with utmost pleasure,
For thou art my greatest treasure.

The time is now
It slips away
I await your second coming,
Be quick my sweet
For soon we'll meet
Our time it is a running.

This second song
that he did sing
Spread smiles to her face,
Her eyes did twinkle with such joy
Whilst her heart pumped on quick pace

He jumped for joy
He sang her name
He twisted with devotion,
She was the fairest of them all
This damsel dipped in potion.

Alas too soon
He jumped for joy
She'd met another suitor,
Yet such was life
For Shaman type
He marched back to his stupa.

There he lies
And there he dies
A traveller breaking through,
Into another region now
He's hardly started to

As for Kara,
Queen of all
She missed her moment too,
The Shaman unlike all the rest
Moves on to places new.

A journey wasted
Means another
For all who sleep so long,
Waking is so hard for them
Unlike the Shaman's song

He blessed her once
Before he left
He stroked her sweet emotion
She was the Queen of all this land
A damsel dipped in potion.

She was the Queen of all this land
A damsel dipped in potion.

She was the Queen of all this land,
A damsel dipped in potion.

the trip

A Vision

The vile stench of man's excesses crawls slowly along the tall
dark tunnels.
Dead lie in the gutter.
Packs of wild dogs scavenge amongst the mountains of
misery,
As she dances along the edge of a blunt knife.

A circle of blood. Warnings, yet not heeded.
Familiar sounds penetrate the circle.
Gratification of abnormal desires. Self-indulgent children.

Dark and desolate, shameful and sad.
Howling terrors rise up from the fathomless abyss.
As a snail leaves a trail,
Man too has an immortal shrine.
Look ahead ! It's not too hard to see.

To Dine with the Devil

I entered the tomb of my mind.
It was time.
Time for realisation.
The dark bleak recesses of thought contained by the
boundless fields of the void.
Lurking incognito behind the shadows,
Lay a familiar figure grinning with the essence of a thousand
demons.
Black and white. Good and Evil.
If good danced in the light
Then a fair assumption was that behind this
Evil smiled with unfathomable attraction.

Drawn helplessly, absorbed by the unknown
I travelled innocently towards my answer.
If one disembowelled good, could it be suggested one was
evil ?
My journey's end, my quest, this would provide the answer I
sought.
A wonderfully fascinating consumption of the mysteries of
the mind.

To play in the fields of the Gods and realise its true identity,
Surely one must first dine with the Devil !

The Sea of Snakes

Diamonds, Rubies and precious stones,
The delights of strange reasoning.
Oh my... how bizarre.
Dancing erratically to an unusual song,
Follow the song, listen to its voice
And rise to its occasion.
Move! Join the path.
The serpent slithers slowly towards the light,
Its skin wrapped smoothly around the toil of man.

Go into the cavern.
The fathomless abyss awaits those who seek the path of the
snake
Go on... Go inside, inside... Go inside.
Come, come inside. Come join us.

The sea of snakes awaits your coming.

The darkness consumes all like a warm blanket of security
Wrapping its long fingers around the neck of mankind.

Seek the cavern!
Seek the Snake!
Join the serpent of your dreams.
Ride forward, swiftly to the delights waiting.
Groovy things happen inside.
Inside, inside, come inside, come on, come inside.
Join us.
The sea of snakes is your coming
The sea of snakes is your coming
The sea of snakes is your coming

Ride the snake
Ride the serpent
Ride the snake
Ride the serpent
Seek its blessing
Seek its life
Seek its soul
Seek its life
Ride the snake
Ride the serpent
Ride, ride, ride !

The sea of snakes awaits.

– CC –